COLOURFUL
SOAP MAKING

Project Book

Learn how to create a
collection of soaps

5 projects inside

INTRODUCTION

Welcome to the world of Soap Making!

This kit has been specifically designed for adults only.

Learning a new skill is always exciting - we're here to help you get started. Anyone can learn how to make soap and with so many options of colours, designs and fragrances as well as a wide range of embellishments such as seeds, dried flowers and more, the only limitation is your imagination.

Whether you're making soap for yourself or as a gift for someone else, there is a great feeling of pride knowing that it's something you have created with your own hands. The good news is, melt and pour soap base sets so quickly, you can start using your new soap straight away.

This kit provides everything you need to make your first soap. There are also four other recipes and step-by-step instructions for you to try. All recipes in this book use melt and pour soap base - there are many places you can buy more supplies to add to your soap making tool kit.

Don't be disheartened if things don't work out the first time. Every skill takes time and effort to master. The most important thing is that you have fun and enjoy yourself. Think about how proud you'll feel when you get to use your very own soap.

Let's begin your soap making journey!

KIT CONTENTS

WHAT'S INCLUDED:

- White Soap base mixture
- Navy blue soap base
- Purple soap base
- Rectangular Soap mould
- Stirring stick

WHAT YOU'LL NEED:

- Microwave or hob for melting soap base
- Microwave safe jug or container
- Heatproof bowl and saucepan with water if using double boiler method
- Tea towel or oven gloves to handle hot containers

It's best to use alcohol spray to ensure you have a smooth finish on your soaps. The rubbing alcohol disperses any bubbles that have formed on the soap with a simple spritz, leaving a shiny smooth surface. The spray needs to be at least 97% alcohol – some hand sanitisers may do the trick

Ingredients:
Hydrogenated Palm Oil, hydrogenated Coconut Oil, Diglycerin, Aqua. Purple CL 77742, Navy CL 77007.

05

MELTING YOUR SOAP

The easiest and quickest way to melt your soap is using a microwave. Place your cut up soap base in a microwave-safe jug or bowl. Place in the microwave and using short bursts of time (depending on how much soap you are using), slowly melt the soap. Check on it regularly until it is entirely melted. Do not allow the soap to boil. This causes air bubbles in your soap – and you don't want that.

The second option is using the double boiler method. Bring two or three inches of water to the boil in a saucepan. Cut up your soap base and place it in a heat proof bowl that is big enough to sit on top of the saucepan. Once the water begins to simmer, place the bowl on the sauce pan. Stir with a spoon or spatula until the soap has melted. The bowl will be hot, be sure to use oven gloves or a towel.

COLOURS

The great thing about soap making is the freedom to choose whatever colours you like. You can have single colour soap, different coloured swirls, multicoloured layers – really, the list is endless.

Test the depth of your colour by using small amounts – if it's liquid, try one drop at a time, if it's powders, try a little bit at the end of a stirring stick – you can add as much or as little as you like until you're satisfied. Food colouring dyes work very well, but always check that your colours can be used in soap.

INGREDIENTS

As with colours, you have many freedoms to choose what ingredients to put in your soap. From dried flowers and seeds, to embeds (small decorations that sit on your soap) and fragrances. essential oils not only make your soap smell delicious but can have great healing properties. There are also many fragrances to choose from that are not essential oils. The standard amount of fragrance to add to your soap is approx. 3%. For example; if you are using 100g of soap, you would add 3g of fragrance. Always check the label on the product you are using for variations.

TIPS & TECHNIQUES:

While it's easy to get excited and want to dive right in, taking time to get prepared will save much frustration later.

Always have everything at hand and ready before you begin to melt the soap. Melt and pour can set really quickly, especially in small amounts. This is not a problem - you can simply melt it again.
The soap base will dry quickly on your spatula – don't waste it. Simply peel it off to use later. You'll be amazed how much left over soap you can save after making several recipes.

Spray your mould with rubbing alcohol just before you pour the soap and immediately after (to get rid of those pesky bubbles). If you are adding another layer, wait until the first pour has set. You don't want to break a layer especially if they are different colours. Spray rubbing alcohol onto the set soap before you pour the next layer. This will help with adhesion between the two layers of soap.

While the soaps in this booklet use only two kinds of moulds, you can use all sorts of shapes and sizes. There are plenty available that are not expensive, or why not do as we did, and use things you can find in your kitchen?*

Find a surface that is easily wiped clean when making your soap.
A chopping board is ideal, because you can also move it around with ease if necessary.

Always keep a damp cloth handy for any drops or spills.

*If items in your kitchen are used in your soap making it is not recommended to use for food preparation.

WARNINGS!

All the makes included in this book are designed specifically for adults.

Keep all ingredients out of the reach of children.

Some ingredients may irritate; always avoid contact with skin and eyes. If ingredients come into contact with eyes or skin, wash with cold water immediately.

Do not ingest; if accidentally ingested drink water and seek medical advice.

We recommend wearing old clothes or overalls when partaking in creative activities. Cover work surfaces to avoid mess.

MARBLE SWIRL

MARBLE SWIRL

In this kit, you can create this beautiful purple marble swirl soap.
Perfect as a gift or just to brighten your bathroom!

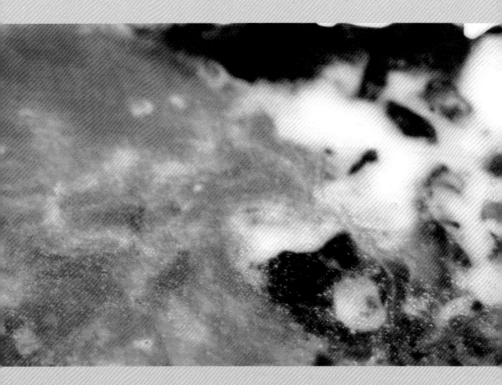

YOU WILL NEED

·Three microwave-safe
containers
·Heat-proof bowls, Pans
and water if using double
boiler method
·Scales
·Rubbing alcohol spray
(optional)

KIT CONTENTS

·Melt and Pour Soap
bases – White, Blue & Purple
·Rectangular Silicone mould
·Stirring stick

METHOD

1. Get organised. Set out all your kit contents on the surface you will be working on. Whether you are using the double boiler method or microwave, it's better to choose an area nearest to the place you will be melting your soap base. (If using the double boiler method, you will need to use three pans and three bowls – these soap bases will need to be melted at the same time.)

2. Place your white soap base in a microwave safe container. It's best to use something small (like a cup), so all three soap bases can fit in the microwave at the same time.

3. Do the same for the blue and purple soap bases.

4. Place the blue, purple and white soap batches in the microwave and melt together. You will only need a very small amount of time. We suggest ten second bursts until the soap is completely melted. Be careful not to let it boil.

5. Spray your mould with rubbing alcohol so it's ready. If the soap has solidified (it will harden very quickly because of the small amounts), put it back in the microwave and melt until liquid again.

6. You will now need to work swiftly, but do not rush. Remove the soap from the microwave and pour the first white layer - about a third of the way into the mould.

7. Immediately afterward, take the blue soap and pour some of it in a swirling motion.

8. Immediately afterward, take the purple soap and pour some of it in a swirling motion.

9. Take the white soap and do the same.

10. Continue to do this until all your soap is used up. If your soap is still fluid, you can swirl a little more with a cocktail stick if you like. Otherwise, spray with rubbing alcohol immediately, to get rid of any bubbles that might form on the surface.

11. Leave the soap to set for 30 minutes. If the soap still feels warm through the mould, it is not ready. Be patient.

12. Once fully set, carefully remove your soap from the mould.

Well Done! You now have your own Purple Swirl soap

CAUTION:

The bowl will be very hot so handle carefully using a tea towel or oven gloves.

15

NOTES

Use the space below to make your own personal notes on the previous project to help when you come back to make it again!

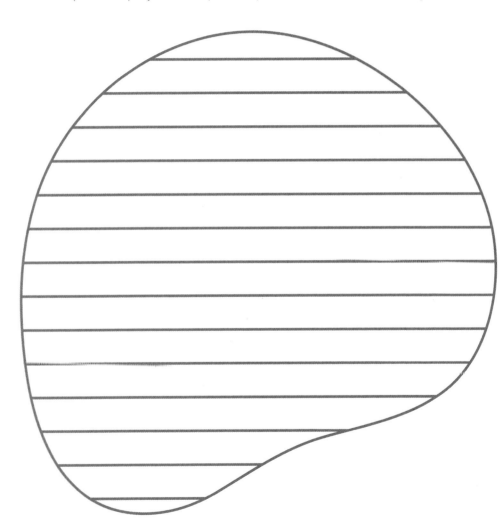

CONFETTI

CONFETTI

Time to celebrate with these cute confetti soaps! Try this new technique by following our instructions below.

YOU WILL NEED

- One or more microwave-safe jug
- Heat-proof bowl, Pan and water if using double boiler method
- Scales
- Grater
- Spatula or wooden spoon
- 2x silicone muffin cases

INGREDIENTS

- 470g of White Soap Base
- Purple dye or colour
- Pink dye or colour

METHOD

1. As mentioned in the Tips and Tricks section, you can use many things for a mould. We found this juice carton was ideal for making a block that cuts easily into three bars of soap. Cut the carton about two thirds of the way down with scissors or a craft knife and discard the top of the carton.

2. To find out how much soap base you need, fill the mould to the desired height with water. Weigh the water in grams. In this recipe, the soap is a little taller, so we have added another 100g to the soap.

3. This soap is going to have six layers of two colours. Split the soap into six equal parts of 75g. (We will be using the remaining 20g later.) If you don't have six jugs or containers, you can always reuse two jugs or containers for the layers. Be certain to keep your white and pink colours separate to produce a striking contrast in the final soap.

4. Place one jug of soap base (75g) in the microwave and using short bursts of 20/30 seconds, melt the soap. Be sure not to let it boil.

5. Pink Layer - Squeeze two or three drops of pink dye into the melted white soap. Do not stir, but using your wrist, create a swirling motion. This will create a swirl in the jug rather than a solid colour.

6. Spray rubbing alcohol in the carton and gently pour the first layer. Spray rubbing alcohol on the layer immediately afterward and leave to set for 10 minutes.

7. Place the next 75g of soap base in a jug and repeat Step 4.

8. White Layer - Ensure the previous layer has hardened by gently pressing your finger on it. There should be a little softness but still firm. Spray the rubbing alcohol on the first layer and pour the second layer. This layer remains white. Spray the rubbing alcohol immediately afterward and leave to set for 10 minutes.

9. Pink Layer - Repeat steps 4 and 5.

10. White Layer - Place the fourth batch of soap base into the microwave and repeat the process of melting it in short bursts of 30 seconds. Making sure the last layer has fully hardened, spray the rubbing alcohol before you pour the white layer. Spray again immediately afterward.

11. Pink Layer – Repeat steps 4 and 5

12. Place the final 75g of soap base in a jug and leave it to the side. In two small containers (silicone muffin cases would be ideal), split the remaining 20g of soap base in two - 10g of soap in each container.

13. Place the cases on a plate or in another container and gently melt the soap, using 10 seconds bursts in the microwave.

14. Carefully take the container out of the microwave once the soap has melted. Squeeze one or two drops of the pink in one case and one or two drops of purple in the other. Stir until mixed and leave to set.

15. Take the hardened soap out of the silicone cases.

16. Using the smallest part of your grater, grate the two colours one after the other so the colours mix in the container beneath. This is the confetti that will sit on top of the final layer.

17. White Layer - Melt the remaining 75g of soap base, ensuring it does not boil. After spraying the last layer with alcohol, pour the final layer of white soap base into the mould.

18. Sprinkle the confetti onto the white layer while it is still fluid and warm, gently pushing it down into the soap so there is a good adhesion. Let the soap set for an hour.

19. Tear the carton gently on all four sides, pulling it to the bottom until you are able to pull the soap free.

20. Slice into bars using a knife or a cheese wire.

Great job. Well done!

CAUTION:

The bowl will be very hot so handle carefully using a tea towel or oven gloves.

NOTES

Use the space below to make your own personal notes on the previous project to help when you come back to make it again!

RAINBOW

RAINBOW

Create a rainbow by following the steps below. Unfortunately, we can't promise a pot of gold at the end.

YOU WILL NEED

- One or more microwave-safe jugs
- Heat-proof bowl, Pan and water if using double boiler method
- Scales
- Spatula or wooden spoon

INGREDIENTS

- 350g of clear soap base
- Purple dye or colour
- Blue dye or colour
- Green dye or colour
- Yellow dye or colour
- Orange dye or colour
- Red dye or colour

METHOD

1. As mentioned already, you can use many things for a mould. We found this juice carton was ideal for making a block that cut easily into three bars of soap. Cut the carton about two thirds of the way down with scissors or a craft knife and discard the top of the carton.

2. To find out how much soap base you need, fill the carton to the desired height with water. Weigh the water in grams. We're cutting this soap across the width, so we do not need it to be as tall as some of the other recipes.

3. This soap is going to have six layers. Split the soap into six equal parts of 58g. If you do not have six containers, reuse one or two jugs. Do make sure you wash them out thoroughly between each layer to ensure you get crisp clean colours.

4. Place your jug of soap base (58g) in the microwave, using 30 second bursts until it is completely melted.

CAUTION:

The bowl will be very hot so handle carefully using a tea towel or oven gloves.

5. Squeeze two drops of purple dye into the soap base and mix thoroughly. Add more drops if you want a deeper colour.

6. Spray rubbing alcohol into the carton and then carefully pour the purple soap for your first layer. Spray rubbing alcohol on the layer immediately afterward. Allow at least 10 minutes for it to set before pouring the next layer.

7. Repeat step 4.

8. Squeeze two drops of blue dye into the melted soap base and mix thoroughly. Spray rubbing alcohol on the previous layer and carefully pour in your blue soap base. Spray rubbing alcohol on the layer immediately afterward. Allow it to set before pouring the next layer.

9. Continue the above steps with the green, yellow, orange and red colour dyes. Be certain that each layer sets before you pour the next. Always remember to spray rubbing alcohol just before and just after you pour each layer.

10. Leave the block of soap to set for an hour.

11. Carefully tear the carton down all four sides until the soap releases.

12. Remove the mould from the ·soap.

13. Cut the soap into bars using a knife or a cheese wire.

Well done! This soap really does shine when placed in direct light!

NOTES

Use the space below to make your own personal notes on the previous project to help when you come back to make it again!

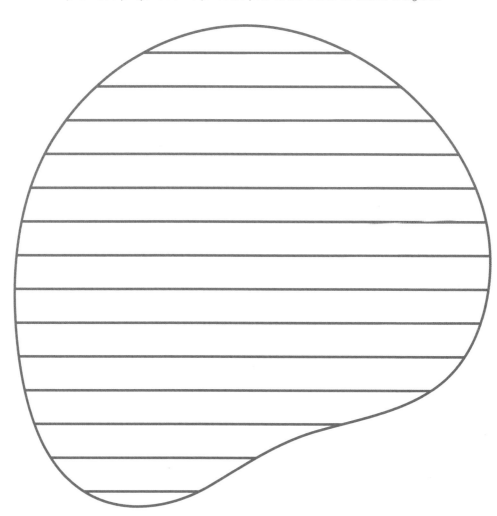

WATERMELON

WATERMELON

Sink your teeth (not literally) into these cute watermelon soaps!
Perfect for a relaxing and refreshing shower!

YOU WILL NEED

· One or more
  microwave-safe jugs
· Heat-proof bowl, pan and
  water if using double
  boiler method
· Scales
· Spatula or wooden spoon
· Rubbing alcohol spray
  (optional)

INGREDIENTS

· 360g of Clear soap base
· 90g of White soap base
· Green dye or colour
· Red dye or colour
· ¼ teaspoon Poppy Seeds

35

METHOD

1. As mentioned already, you can use many things for a mould. We found this juice carton was ideal for making a block that cut easily into three bars of soap. Cut the carton about two thirds of the way down with scissors or a craft knife and discard the top of the carton.

2. Measure 112g of the clear soap base. Cut it into cubes this will help it to melt quicker. Place the soap base in a microwave safe jug and microwave on short bursts of 30 seconds until it is completely melted.

3. Squeeze three drops of green dye into the soap base and mix thoroughly.

4. Spray rubbing alcohol into the mould and carefully pour in the soap base. Spray rubbing alcohol onto the layer immediately after pouring. Wait until the layer is set (10 mins) before pouring the next layer.

5. Place the white soap base (90g) in a microwave-safe jug. Melt in the microwave using short bursts of 30 seconds until melted.

CAUTION:

The bowl will be very hot so handle carefully using a tea towel or oven gloves.

6. Remove the white soap from the microwave when melted. Spray green layer with rubbing alcohol, and carefully pour the white soap base into the mould. Spraying again immediately afterward.

7. Place the remaining clear soap base (225g) in a microwave-safe jug. Put in the microwave for short bursts of 30 seconds until melted.

8. Remove from the microwave and add three drops of red dye to your melted soap base. Stir until the dye is fully mixed. If you want more depth to your soap base, add more colour, one drop at a time.

9. Add ¼ teaspoon of poppy seeds to your soap.

10. Stir well until fully mixed

11. Spray the white layer with rubbing alcohol and carefully pour the red soap base into the mould.

12. Leave the soap to set for at least an hour.

13. Carefully tear the carton on each of its sides until the soap becomes free.

14. Remove the Watermelon soap from the mould.

15. Cut your soap into bars using a knife or cheese wire.

These soaps look quite stunning when placed in direct light.

TIP: You can add a watermelon fragrance! See page 7.

NOTES

Use the space below to make your own personal notes on the previous project to help when you come back to make it again!

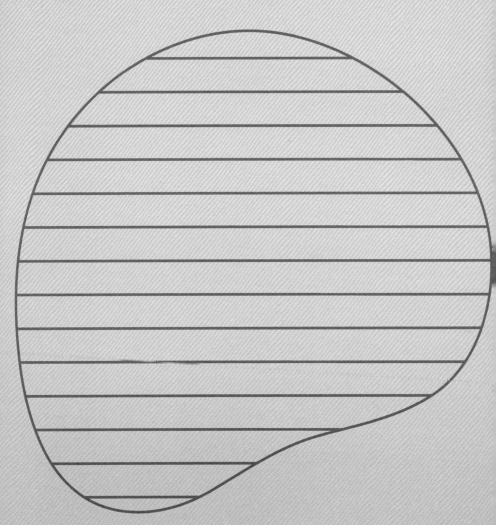

OMBRE

OMBRE

Create this beautiful ombre soap using the step by step below. Choose your favourite colours, match your decor or even create for a friend!

YOU WILL NEED

· One or more microwave-safe jugs
· Heat-proof bowl, pan and water if using double boiler method
· Scales
· Spatula or wooden spoon

INGREDIENTS

· 70g of Clear soap base
· 30g of White soap base
· Blue dye or colour
· Pink dye or colour

METHOD

1. Get all your items together on the surface you will be working on. Find a thin book and rest your soap up against it. You can experiment with how far your soap will travel up the mould using water before you begin. You want the angle to allow the water to almost reach the opposite edge, but not quite.

2. Split your clear soap base in half so you have two batches of soap base. 35g each.

3. Melt the first jug of clear soap base (35g) in the microwave. Use small bursts of 10 seconds until fully melted – it's a small amount of soap – don't let it boil.

4. Add one drop of blue dye to the melted soap base. Add more if necessary, depending on how deep you want your colour to look.

5. Stir until the colour is mixed thoroughly.

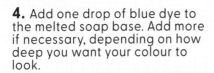

6. Spray the silicone mould with rubbing alcohol. Carefully pour the soap base into the mould until it almost reaches the other end, but not quite. Such small amounts of soap will harden quickly. Spray the rubbing alcohol on the layer immediately after pouring.

7. Wait until this layer sets completely (10 mins). Pouring before the soap has hardened will break the layer beneath and ruin the ombre effect. Be patient. Once the layer has set, turn the mould 180 degrees, and position it back onto the thin book.

8. Melt the second jug of clear soap base (35g) in the microwave. Use small bursts of 10 seconds to ensure the soap does not boil.

9. Add one drop of pink dye to the melted soap. As with the blue – if you desire a deeper colour, add more drops as necessary.

10. Stir well until the colour is mixed completely.

11. Spray the blue layer with rubbing alcohol and carefully pour the pink layer into the mould. Such small amounts of soap will harden quickly. Spray the rubbing alcohol on the pink layer immediately after pouring. Leave to set for 10 minutes or more.

12. Place your white soap base (30g) into a microwave-safe jug and melt in the microwave. Use ten second bursts and do not allow it to boil.

13. Making sure the previous layer is entirely set (you can do this by gently pressing on it with your fingers), spray rubbing alcohol onto the pink layer. Make sure this is now on a flat surface then carefully pour all of the white soap base into the mould. Spray with rubbing alcohol immediately

14. Wait for 30 minutes or until the soap is fully set. If it's still warm to the touch through the mould, it's not ready. Be patient.

15. Carefully remove the mould from your soap.

Well done! You now have a beautiful Ombre soap.

CAUTION:
The bowl will be very hot so handle carefully using a tea towel or oven gloves.

NOTES

Use the space below to make your own personal notes on the previous project to help when you come back to make it again!